Jane Yolen's
Mother Goose Songbook

SELECTED, EDITED, AND INTRODUCED BY

Jane Yolen

MUSICAL ARRANGEMENTS BY

Adam Stemple

ILLUSTRATIONS BY

Rosekrans Hoffman

Jane Yolen's Mother Goose Songbook

CAROLINE HOUSE　BOYDS MILLS PRESS

Text copyright © 1992 by Jane Yolen
Musical arrangements © 1992 by Adam Stemple
Illustrations copyright © 1992 by Rosekrans Hoffman

Published by Caroline House
Boyds Mills Press, Inc.
A Highlights Company
910 Church Street
Honesdale, Pennsylvania 18431

Publisher Cataloging-in-Publication Data
Main entry under title.
Jane Yolen's Mother Goose Songbook / musical arrangements by
Adam Stemple ; illustrations by Rosekrans Hoffman.—1st ed.
[96] p. : col. ill. ; cm.
Includes index.
Summary: Music accompanies familiar nursery rhymes.
ISBN 1-878093-52-5
[1. Nursery rhymes.] I. Mother Goose. II. Yolen, Jane. III. Stemple, Adam.
IV. Hoffman, Rosekrans. V. Title.
398.8—dc20   1992
Library of Congress Catalog Card Number: 91-77616

First edition, 1992
Book designed by Joy Chu
The text of this book is set in 12-point Bodoni; the song lyrics are set in
10.5-point Bodoni. The display types are Announcement Italic and Cochin Roman.
The illustrations are colored inks.
Distributed by St. Martin's Press
Printed in Hong Kong

10 9 8 7 6 5 4 3 2

Acknowledgments: Much of the information about the
rhymes comes from the following sources—The Annotated
Mother Goose by William S. Baring-Gould and Ceil
Baring-Gould; Popular Rhymes and Nursery Tales by
James Orchard Halliwell-Phillips; Nursery Rhymes and
Tales by Henry Bett; and Counting-Out Rhymes by Roger D.
Abrahams and Lois Rankin.

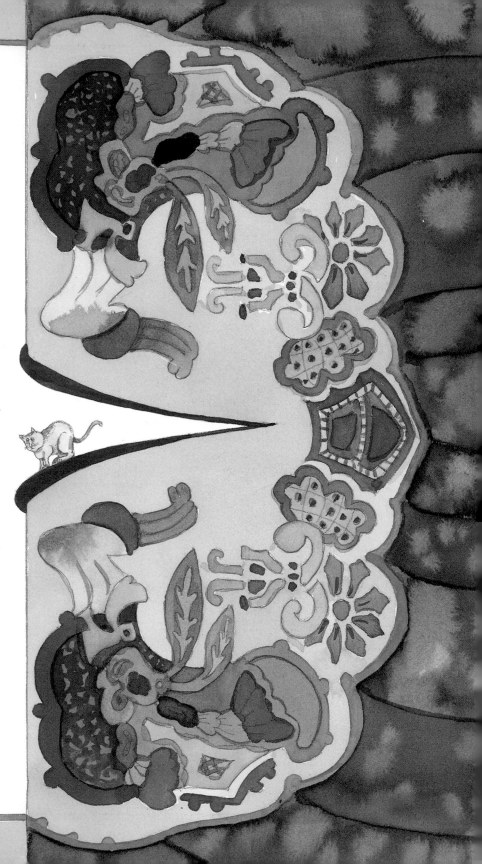

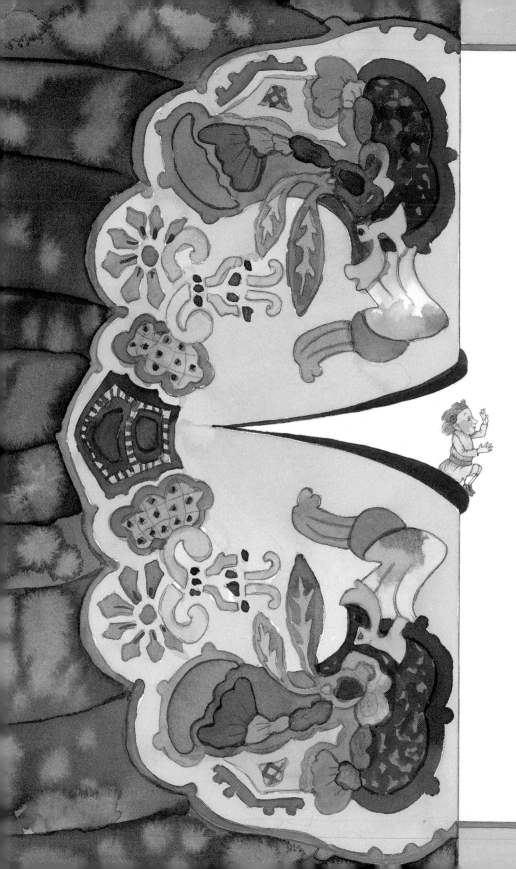

To my three children,
HEIDI, ADAM, and JASON,
and their children to come—JY

For LORRAINE—AS

To LIBBY—RH

Contents

Singing Mother Goose

MOTHER GOOSE, that quiet grande dame of the nursery set, has as complicated a lineage as any pretender to a royal throne. And if her rhymes seem the safe, sane, and perfect nonsense for little tongues, mothers and fathers may be surprised to find that what appear to be lullabies and fingerplays, silly rhymes and jolly nonsense were once political satire or relics of ancient rituals.

How did these things sneak into the nursery? Quite simply. Children have always been great listeners and masters of eavesdropping. As time went on, they liked the rhymes, cared little for the sense, and took them for their own. The rhymes have long outlived their political or ritual meanings.

Over the centuries, a certain body of work has come to be called "Mother Goose" rhymes. But the first reference to Mother Goose in literature was as a teller of stories in a French poem written in 1650, long after many of these rhymes first appeared. In 1697 Mother Goose's name was attached to Charles Perrault's classic collection of fairy tales: *Contes de ma mère l'Oye*. The first edition of that book has a frontispiece showing an old woman at a spinning wheel, presumably also spinning stories to a man, a girl, a little boy, and a cat.

Old Mother Goose was not connected to nursery verse until 1760, when a little book called *Mother Goose's Melody* was published in London by John Newbery, whose name is identified with the highest award given to an American children's book, the Newbery Medal.

Mother Goose's Melody contained both rhymes and adult commentary and was so popular that the books were simply loved to pieces by their owners. Today there is no known complete copy of the book.

Mother Goose traveled to America in the arms of a literary pirate, Isaiah Thomas. He had been a boy when the original *Melody* had come out. When he grew up, Thomas became a printer, and he took advantage of the fact that America was at war with England. He smuggled a number of Newbery's books to the rebellious colonies and printed his own versions. He made a fortune.

Boston, Massachusetts, has its own claim to Mother Goose: Mistress Vergoose, mother-in-law of printer Thomas Fleet, who collected the rhymes she told her children and grandchildren in *Songs of the Nursery*, published in 1719.

Many of the rhymes had been sung for centuries, some chanted as weather rituals or love tokens. Others were set to traditional songs, folk music, marching songs, and the like. Still others were composed songs by popular musicians of the day. Even Wolfgang Amadeus Mozart composed nursery songs, like "Twinkle, Twinkle, Little Star."

I have chosen those songs that I heard from my own mother and passed on to my three children. My son, Adam Stemple, has put them into simple piano arrangements with guitar chords as well. And so these songs travel on, from our family to yours, not mouth to ear, the old way, but on the pages of a book.

Still, as Mother Goose said in *The Only True Mother Goose Melodies*, published in 1843:

No, no, my melodies will never die,
While nurses sing and babies cry.

—Jane Yolen

This Little Pig

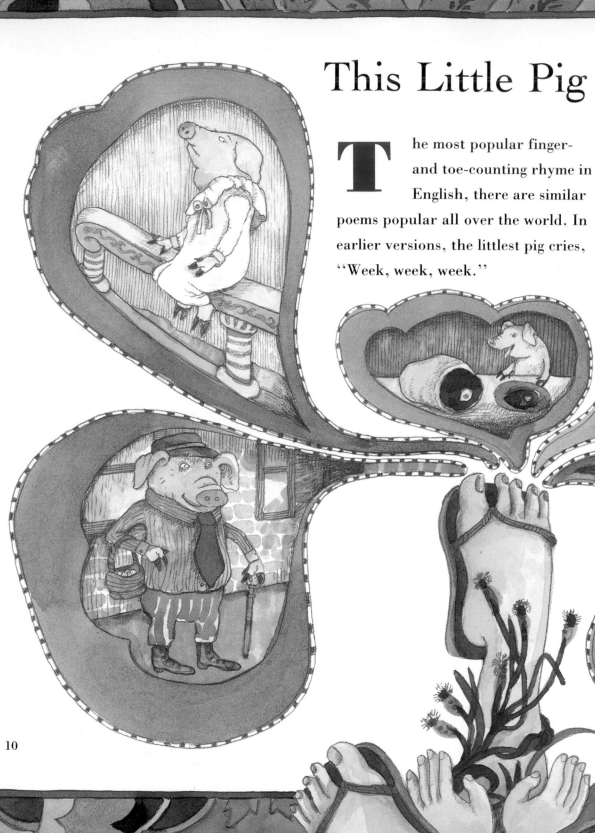

The most popular finger- and toe-counting rhyme in English, there are similar poems popular all over the world. In earlier versions, the littlest pig cries, "Week, week, week."

10

Gaily

This lit - tle pig went to mar - ket, This lit - tle pig stayed home; _____

This lit - tle pig had roast beef, This lit - tle pig had none; ___

This lit - tle pig cried, "Wee, wee, wee," All _____ the way home.

Bobby Shafto

Bobby Shafto is known by other names: Willy Foster, Bobby Shaft, Billy Button. The original Bobby Shafto is said to have lived in Hollybrook, County Wicklow, in Ireland, and died in 1737. When a different Bobby Shafto ran for Parliament in 1761, his supporters sang this song during his campaign.

Softly

1. Bob - by Shaf - to went to sea, Sil - ver buck - les on his knee,

He'll come back and mar - ry me, ___ Pret - ty Bob - by Shaf - to.

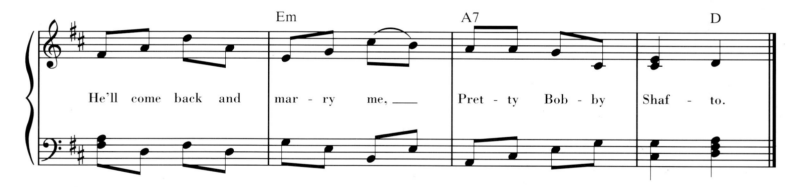

2. Bobby Shafto's fat and fair,

Combing down his yellow hair,

He's my love for evermore,

Pretty Bobby Shafto.

13

Polly, Put the Kettle On

 riginally a country dance and song, the verse migrated to the nursery in the 19th century. It was so well known that Charles Dickens, the popular British novelist, had a raven croak, "Polly, put the kettle on and we'll all have tea," in *Barnaby Rudge*.

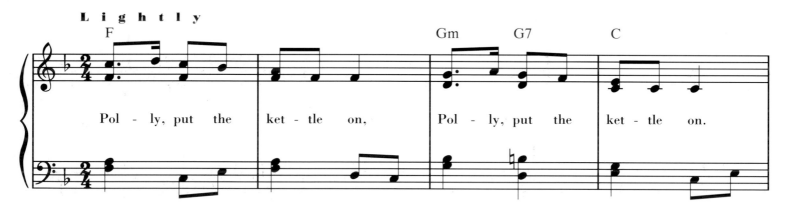

Polly, put the kettle on, Polly, put the kettle on.

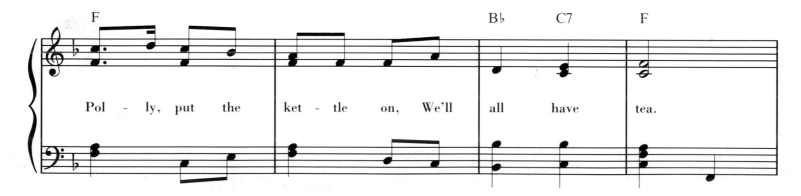

Polly, put the kettle on, We'll all have tea.

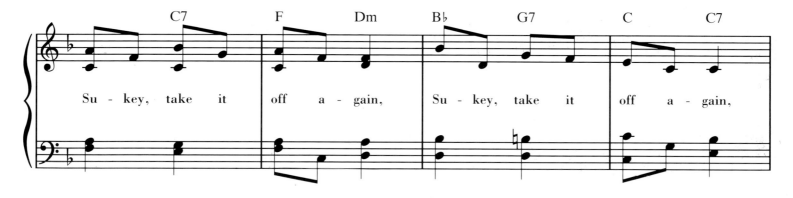

Su - key, take it off a - gain, Su - key, take it off a - gain,

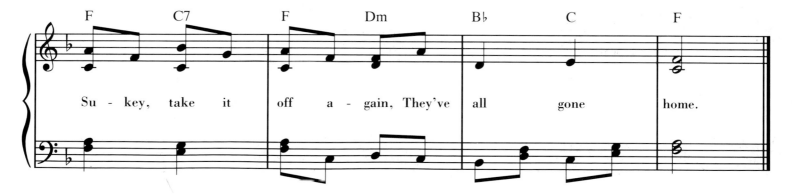

Su - key, take it off a - gain, They've all gone home.

Aiken Drum

This Scottish song can be found in many versions. The name Aiken Drum was given to the Brownie of Blednoch in Galloway by the poet William Nicholson in 1878, but this song had been printed in a nursery rhyme collection some 20 years earlier. *Haggis* is a food peculiar to Scotland.

Quickly

1. There ___ was a man lived in the moon, lived in the moon, lived

in the moon. There __ was a man lived in the moon, and his name was Ai - ken

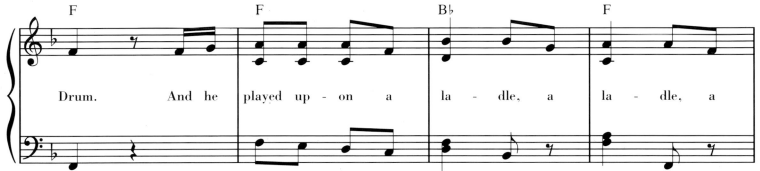

Drum. And he played up - on a la - dle, a la - dle, a

la - dle, And he played up - on a la - dle and his name was Ai - ken Drum.

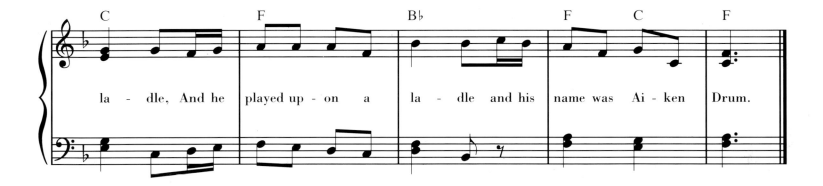

2.

And his hat was made of good cream cheese,

Of good cream cheese, of good cream cheese.

And his hat was made of good cream cheese,

And his name was Aiken Drum. (*Chorus*)

3.

And his coat was made of good roast beef,

Of good roast beef, of good roast beef.

And his coat was made of good roast beef,

And his name was Aiken Drum. (*Chorus*)

4.

And his breeches made of haggis bags,

Of haggis bags, of haggis bags.

And his breeches made of haggis bags,

And his name was Aiken Drum. (*Chorus*)

17

Froggie Went A-Courting

Mentioned in an English play in 1549, this song made its first full appearance as "A Moste Strange Wedding of the Frogge and the Mowse." There are hundreds of versions in America and Britain.

Playfully

1. ___ Frog-gie went a-court-ing and he did ride, a - hum, a - hum.
2. He rode ___ up ___ to ___ Miss Mous-ie's door, a - hum, a - hum.

1. Frog-gie went a-court-ing and he did ride, a - hum, a - hum.
2. He rode ___ up ___ to ___ Miss Mous-ie's door, a - hum, a - hum.

1. Frog-gie went a-court-ing and he did ride, A sword and pis - tol by his side, A -
2. He rode ___ up ___ to ___ Miss Mous-ie's door, Where he had been many times be - fore, A -

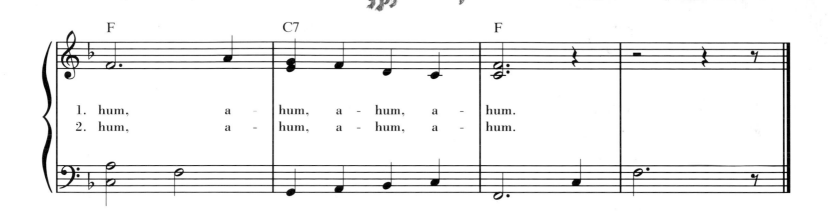

F   C7   F

1. hum,   a - hum,   a - hum,   a - hum.
2. hum,   a - hum,   a - hum,   a - hum.

3. He said, "Miss Mouse, are you within?" a-hum, a-hum.

   He said, "Miss Mouse, are you within?" a-hum, a-hum.

   He said, "Miss Mouse, are you within?"

   She said, "I sit by the fire and spin."

   A-hum, a-hum, a-hum, a-hum.

4. He said, "Miss Mouse, will you marry me?" a-hum, a-hum.

   He said, "Miss Mouse, will you marry me?" a-hum, a-hum.

   He said, "Miss Mouse, will you marry me?"

   She said, "If Uncle Rat will agree."

   A-hum, a-hum, a-hum, a-hum.

5. "Where will the wedding supper be?" a-hum, a-hum.

   "Where will the wedding supper be?" a-hum, a-hum.

   "Where will the wedding supper be?"

   "Out in the woods in a hollow tree."

   A-hum, a-hum, a-hum, a-hum.

6. Just as they were sitting to sup, a-hum, a-hum.

   Just as they were sitting to sup, a-hum, a-hum.

   Just as they were sitting to sup,

   Along came a cat and go-bobbled them up.

   A-hum, a-hum, a-hum, a-hum.

7. That's the end of those all three, a-hum, a-hum.

   That's the end of those all three, a-hum, a-hum.

   That's the end of those all three,

   The frog, the rat, and the little mousie,

   A-hum, a-hum, a-hum, a-hum.

8. There's bread and cheese upon the shelf, a-hum, a-hum.

   There's bread and cheese upon the shelf, a-hum, a-hum.

   There's bread and cheese upon the shelf,

   If you want any more you can sing it yourself.

   A-hum, a-hum, a-hum, a-hum.

19

The Farmer's in the Dell

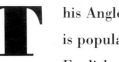

This Anglo-American song is popular throughout the English-speaking world. It has changed in the American Midwest into a counting-out rhyme, "The Farmer's in the Den."

With good humor

1. The farm-er's in the dell, The farm-er's in the dell,

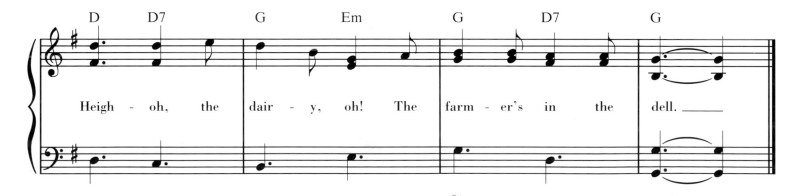

Heigh - oh, the dair - y, oh! The farm-er's in the dell. _____

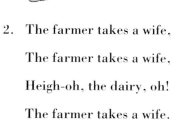

2. The farmer takes a wife,
    The farmer takes a wife,
    Heigh-oh, the dairy, oh!
    The farmer takes a wife.

5. The cat takes a rat,
    The cat takes a rat,
    Heigh-oh, the dairy, oh!
    The cat takes a rat.

3. The wife takes a child,
    The wife takes a child,
    Heigh-oh, the dairy, oh!
    The wife takes a child.

6. The rat takes the cheese,
    The rat takes the cheese,
    Heigh-oh, the dairy, oh!
    The rat takes the cheese.

4. The child takes a cat,
    The child takes a cat,
    Heigh-oh, the dairy, oh!
    The child takes a cat.

7. And the cheese stands alone,
    The cheese stands alone,
    Heigh-oh, the dairy, oh!
    The cheese stands alone.

Fiddle-De-De

Based on an old nursery rhyme, this New England version was collected by England's popular "Father Goose," James O. Halliwell-Phillips, in the early 19th century.

With a lilt

1. Fid-dle-de-de, fid-dle-de-de, The fly has mar-ried the bum-ble-bee. Says the fly, says he, "Will you mar-ry me And live with me, sweet bum-ble-bee?"

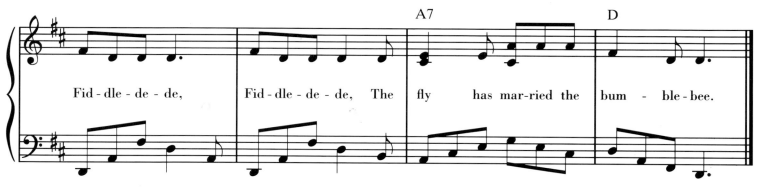

Fid - dle - de - de, Fid - dle - de - de, The fly has mar-ried the bum - ble - bee.

2. Fiddle-de-de, fiddle-de-de,

   The fly has married the bumblebee,

   Says the bee, says she, "I'll live under your wing,

   And you'll never know I carry a sting."

   Fiddle-de-de, fiddle-de-de,

   The fly has married the bumblebee.

3. Fiddle-de-de, fiddle-de-de,

   The fly has married the bumblebee.

   So when parson beetle he joined the pair,

   They both took off to take the air.

   Fiddle-de-de, fiddle-de-de,

   The fly has married the bumblebee.

4. Fiddle-de-de, fiddle-de-de,

   The fly has married the bumblebee.

   Oh, the flies did buzz and the bells did ring.

   Did you ever hear a merrier thing?

   Fiddle-de-de, fiddle-de-de,

   The fly has married the bumblebee.

Goosey, Goosey, Gander

This 18th-century street rhyme celebrated a terrible murder, when Cardinal Beaton was thrown down a set of stairs for not saying the prayers insisted on by the new rulers of England.

24

Flowingly

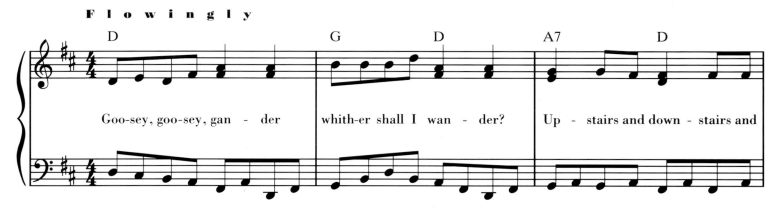

Goo-sey, goo-sey, gan - der whith-er shall I wan - der? Up - stairs and down - stairs and

in my la - dy's cham - ber. There I met an old man who would not say his prayers. I took

him by the left leg and ___ threw him down the stairs.

25

Here We Go 'Round the Mulberry Bush

C hildren sang this little tune in the 18th century. There is a popular ring game that goes along with it. The British version uses the term "bramble bush."

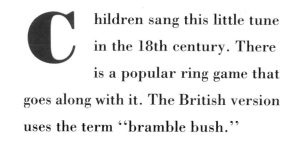

With a happy bounce

1. Here we go 'round the mul-ber-ry bush, the mul-ber-ry bush, the mul-ber-ry bush,

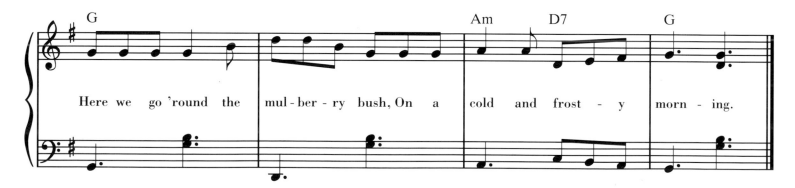

Here we go 'round the mul-ber-ry bush, On a cold and frost-y morn-ing.

26

2. This is the way we wash our hands,
   Wash our hands, wash our hands,
   This is the way we wash our hands,
   On a cold and frosty morning.

3. This is the way we clean our rooms,
   Clean our rooms, clean our rooms,
   This is the way we clean our rooms,
   On a cold and frosty morning.

Hey, Diddle, Diddle

According to some scholars, this is the best-known nonsense verse in the English language and possibly refers to England's Queen Elizabeth I dancing with her friends at court.

With a bounce

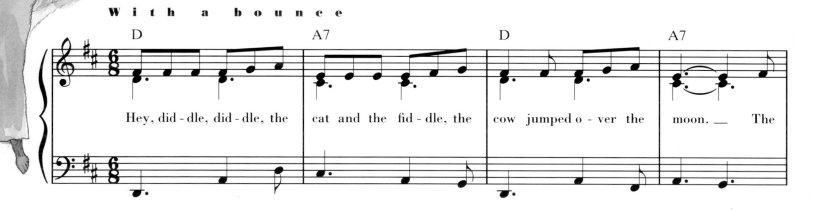

Hey, did - dle, did - dle, the cat and the fid - dle, the cow jumped o - ver the moon. ___ The

lit - tle dog laughed_ to see such sport, And the dish ran a - way with the spoon. ___

Humpty Dumpty

The first time this popular rhyme was printed was in *Gammer Gurton's Garland* in 1810. By the time Lewis Carroll used the figure of Humpty Dumpty in his book *Through the Looking Glass*, 50 years later, no one had any doubt Humpty was an egg.

Sprightly

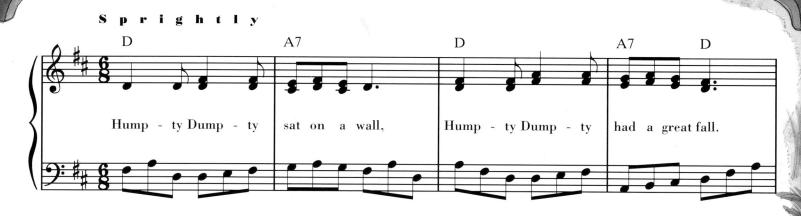

Hump – ty Dump – ty sat on a wall, Hump – ty Dump – ty had a great fall.

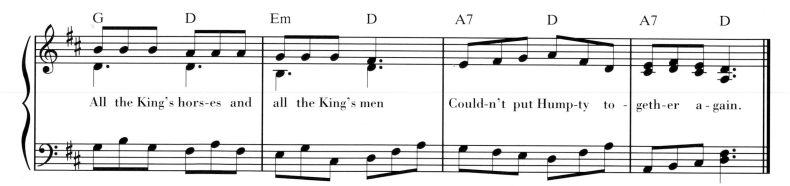

All the King's hors-es and all the King's men Could-n't put Hump-ty to – geth-er a – gain.

I Love Little Pussy

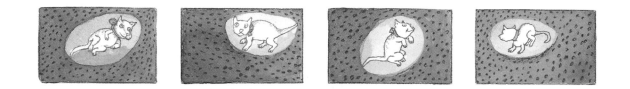

I n the first printing of this song, in *The Only True Mother Goose Melodies* in 1843, there was a different last line: "So I'll not pull her tail,

Nor drive her away, But pussy and I, Very gently will play." In the earlier version, the singer said only, "I *like* little pussy."

S w e e t l y

| Bb | Eb6 | F7 | Bb |

I __ love lit-tle puss-y her coat is so warm, And __ if I don't hurt her, she'll do me no harm. I'll __

| | Eb6 | F7 | Bb |

sit by the fire __ and give her some food, And __ puss-y will love me be-cause I am good.

Lady Bird, Lady Bird

According to folk tradition, it is unlucky to kill a lady bird or—as it is known in America—a ladybug. Rather, one should encourage it to "fly away home." The song itself is probably left over from an old European luck or weather ritual, for the insect's name is a contraction of "Our Lady's Bird."

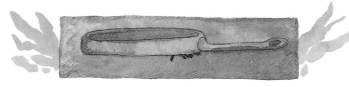

Quietly

Lady bird, lady bird fly a-way home. Your house is on fire, __ your chil-dren are gone.

All __ but one and her name __ is Ann, And she __ hid un-der the fry - ing pan.

31

Baa, Baa, Black Sheep

More than 200 years old, this English song may be about the wool tax— given to the King (master) and the nobility (Dame) by the sheep farmers (the little boy in the lane).

Baa, baa, black sheep, have you an - y wool? Yes, sir, yes, sir, three bags full.

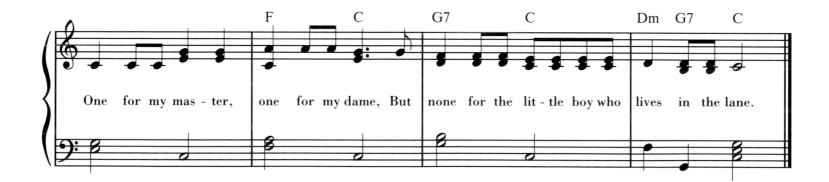

One for my mas - ter, one for my dame, But none for the lit - tle boy who lives in the lane.

32

Georgy Porgy

lso known as Charley Barley or Rowley Powley, Georgy Porgy has been playing tricks for 150 years.

It is said that the original of Georgy was either King George I of England or King Charles II of England, both popular with the ladies.

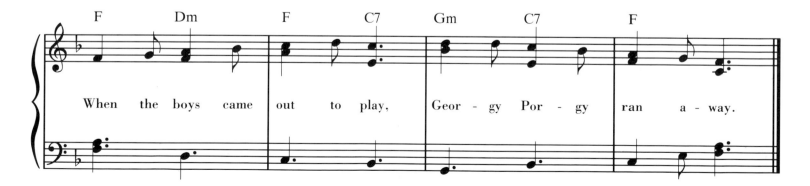

Liltingly

Geor - gy Por - gy, pud - ding and pie, Kissed the girls and made them cry.

When the boys came out to play, Geor - gy Por - gy ran a - way.

Little Bo-Peep

The earliest printed version of this most popular nursery song is in *Gammer Gurton's Garland* in 1810, though there is a peek-a-boo game of that name mentioned as early as 1364. And there was a court game known as "boe-pepe" at the time of Queen Elizabeth I. Spelling had not been regularized at that time.

Lightly

C   G   G7   C   G7   C

1. Lit - tle Bo - Peep has lost her sheep, And can't tell where __ to find them;

F   C   Dm   G7   D#dim   C   G7   C

Leave them a - lone, and they'll come home, Wag-ging their tails __ be - hind them.

2. Little Bo-Peep fell fast asleep,

   And dreamed she heard them bleating;

   But when she woke, 'twas all a joke,

   For they were still a-fleeting.

3. Then up she took her little crook,

   Determined for to find them;

   She found them indeed, but her heart did bleed,

   They'd left all their tails behind them.

4. Heaving a sigh, she wiped her eye,

   And over the hills went stump-o;

   Tried what she could as a shepherdess should,

   And tacked up each tail to each rump-o.

Jack and Jill

Originally a British political rhyme from the 18th century, this verse, when first printed, was accompanied by a woodcut showing two boys, and the title was *Jack and Gill.*

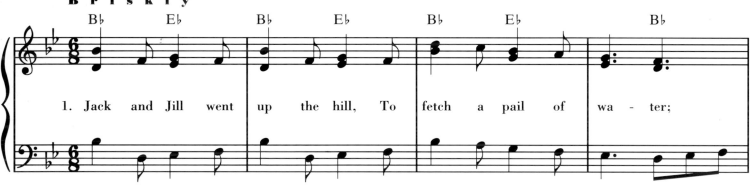

Briskly

Bb   Eb   Bb   Eb   Bb   Eb   Bb

1. Jack and Jill went up the hill, To fetch a pail of wa - ter;

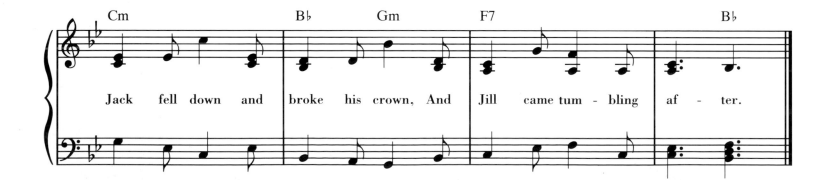

Cm   Bb   Gm   F7   Bb

Jack fell down and broke his crown, And Jill came tum - bling af - ter.

2. Then up Jack got, and home did trot

   As fast as he could caper,

   To old Dame Dob, who patched his nob

   With vinegar and brown paper.

3. Then Jill came in, and she did grin

   To see Jack's paper plaster;

   Dame Dob, vexed, did whip her next

   For causing Jack's disaster.

37

Lavender's Blue

This nursery song, a version of which was first printed between 1672 and 1685, is really a shortened form of an old ballad, "Diddle, Diddle, Or The Kind Country Lovers." A pop version sung by Dinah Shore was a hit in both England and America in 1948.

Sweetly

1. Lav - en - der's blue, dil - ly, dil - ly, lav - en - der's green;

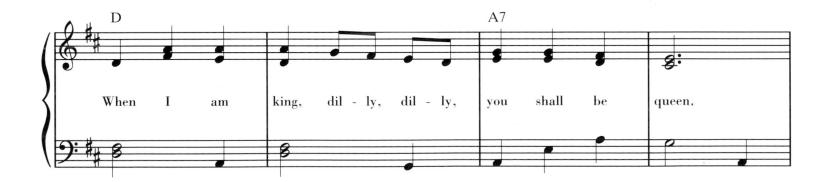

When I am king, dil - ly, dil - ly, you shall be queen,

D   G   Em

Who told you so, dil - ly, dil - ly, who told you so?

D   A7   D

'Twas my own heart, dil - ly, dil - ly, that told me so.

2. Call up your men, dilly, dilly, set them to work;

Some to the plough, dilly, dilly, some to the cart.

Some to make hay, dilly, dilly, some to cut corn;

Whilst you and I, dilly, dilly, keep ourselves warm.

Lazy Mary

Whether it is Mary or Molly or Polly who is named as the lazy girl, this song is popular in both England and America.

With spirit

1. La - zy Mar - y, will you get up, Will you get up, will you get up?

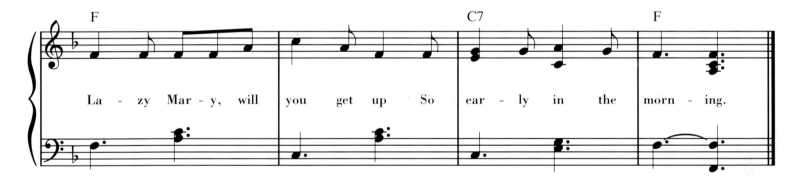

La - zy Mar - y, will you get up So ear - ly in the morn - ing.

2. No, no, mother, I won't get up,
   I won't get up, I won't get up,
   No, no, mother, I won't get up
   So early in the morning.

41

Cock-a-Doodle-Doo!

The earliest version of this popular English nursery song comes from the book *Mother Goose's Melody*, printed in the 1760s. But possibly it is much older, since two lines from the rhyme appeared in a 1606 pamphlet about a murder.

Brightly

1. Cock - a - doo - dle - doo! ____ My dame has lost her shoe, ____ My

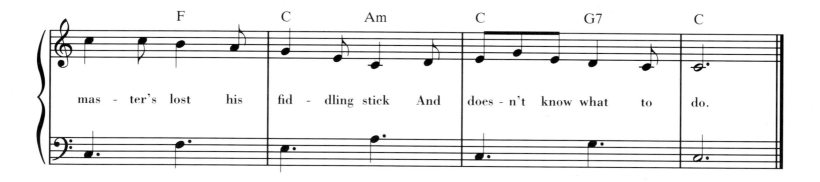

mas - ter's lost his fid - dling stick And does - n't know what to do.

2. Cock-a-doo-dle-doo!

What is my dame to do?

Till Master finds his fiddling stick

She'll dance without her shoe.

43

Little Boy Blue

Nursery rhyme scholars quarrel over the origin of this simple rhyme. Some feel it is a political verse about Thomas, Cardinal Wolsey, chief minister for King Henry VIII. Others think it refers to a speech in Shakespeare's *King Lear*.

Sweetly

Lit - tle Boy Blue, come blow your horn, The sheep's in the mea-dow, the cow's in the corn.

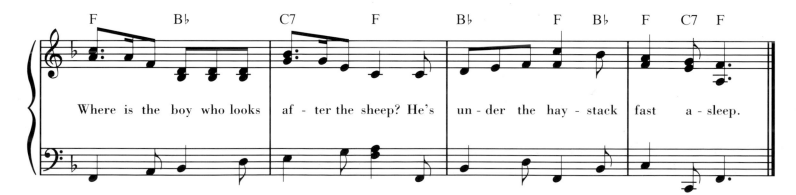

Where is the boy who looks af - ter the sheep? He's un - der the hay - stack fast a - sleep.

Little Jack Horner

The earliest printed version of this British political rhyme was in the ballad "Namby Pamby" by Henry Carey in 1720. It appeared in a nursery rhyme book some 40 years later. Supposedly the verse celebrates one Thomas Horner, a steward to the last abbot of Glastonbury Cathedral. The abbot sent Horner with a pie baked with deeds for 12 large estates to be given to King Henry VIII. On the way, Horner stole one of the deeds. His descendants still live in that mansion.

With gentle humor

Lit - tle Jack Hor - ner sat in a cor - ner, Eat - ing his Christ - mas pie. _____ He

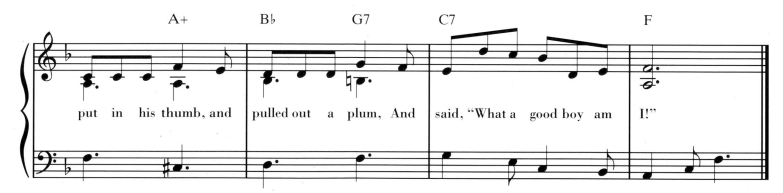

put in his thumb, and pulled out a plum, And said, "What a good boy am I!"

The Muffin Man

There was a Muffin Man who used to sell his wares on British street corners. Drury Lane is in London.

With a bounce

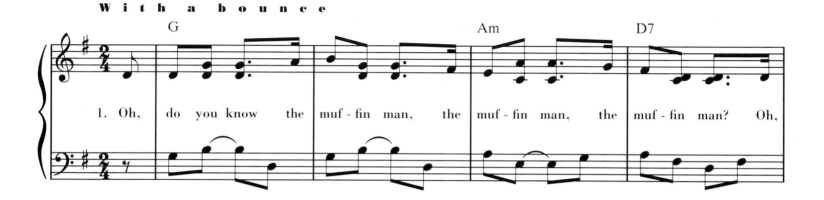

1. Oh, do you know the muf-fin man, the muf-fin man, the muf-fin man? Oh,

do you know the muf-fin man Who lives in Dru-ry Lane?

2. Oh, yes, I know the muffin man,
The muffin man, the muffin man.
Oh, yes, I know the muffin man
Who lives in Drury Lane.

47

Little Tommy Tucker

Tom Tucker is a very old Scottish phrase meaning a person who takes things for himself at the expense of others.

To "sing for one's supper" comes from the days when minstrels went from houses to castles to inns and sang in exchange for food and a bed.

Charmingly

Lit-tle Tom-my Tuck-er | Sings for his sup-per. | What shall he sing for? | White bread and but-ter.

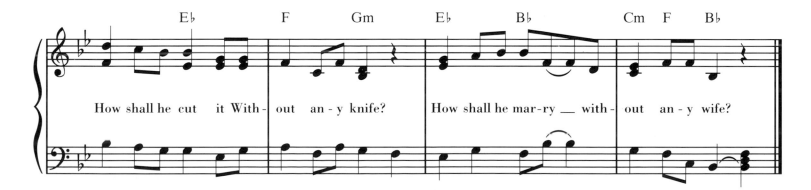

How shall he cut it With-out an-y knife? | How shall he mar-ry __ with-out an-y wife?

48

Pussy Cat, Pussy Cat

First printed as a rhyme in
1805, the verse celebrates
a much earlier time. The
queen is supposed to be Elizabeth I of
England, and the rhyme is about the
time she found a mouse in the folds of
her dress.

Softly

E   B

Puss-y cat, puss-y cat, | where have you been? | I've been to Lon-don to | vis - it the Queen.

C#m   B   E   A   F#m   E   B7   E

Puss-y cat, puss-y cat, | what did you there? I | fright-ened a lit - tle mouse | un-der her chair.

Pop! Goes the Weasel

Originally a 17th-century British children's song, it was printed in a broadside in 1855 with many new verses. In America it became popular as a square-dance tune. "The weasel" is a nickname for a cobbler's tool. To "pop" the weasel meant to pawn that tool for money.

With gusto

All a-round the cob - bler's bench, The mon - key chased the wea - sel. The

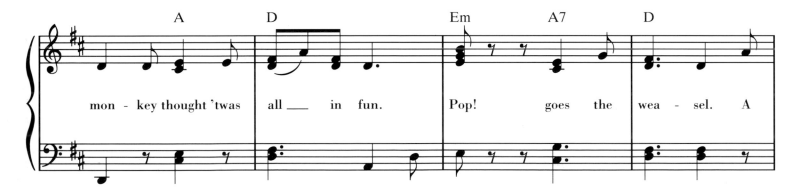

mon - key thought 'twas all ___ in fun. Pop! goes the wea - sel. A

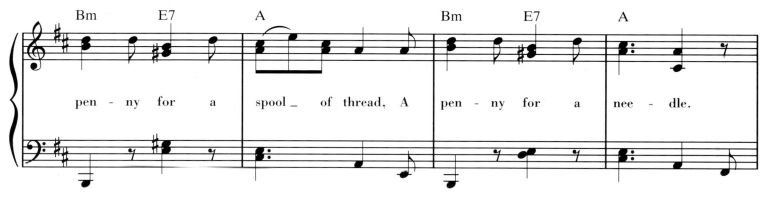

pen - ny for a spool __ of thread, A pen - ny for a nee - dle.

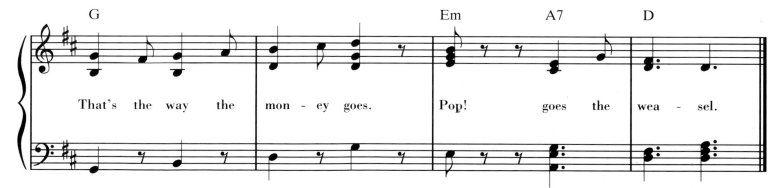

That's the way the mon - ey goes. Pop! goes the wea - sel.

Ring Around a Rosy

Also known as "Ring-a-Ring o' Roses," this British singing game first saw print in Kate Greenaway's *Mother Goose* in 1881. A persistent popular view is that this rhyme pertains to the Great Plague: the roses refer to the rosy rash, posies to flowers carried to ward off the smell of death, and ashes and falling down to the plague years. Most scholars nowadays dismiss this theory.

In a sing-song manner

Ring a-round a ros-y, a pock-et full of po-sies.

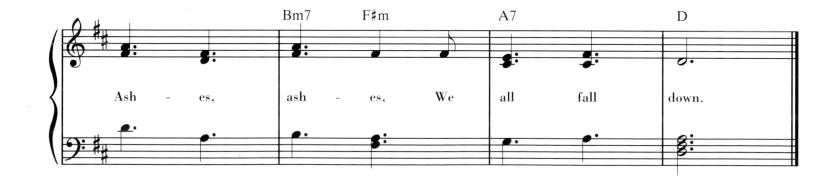

Ash-es, ash-es, We all fall down.

Row, Row, Row Your Boat

A four-part round, this simple song is an American nursery favorite, probably written in the 19th century. The poet is unknown.

Smoothly

Row, row, row your boat Gen-tly down the stream.

Mer-ri-ly, mer-ri-ly, mer-ri-ly, mer-ri-ly, Life is but a dream.

Sing a Song of Sixpence

There exist several theories about this song. Some scholars think it has to do with the 24 hours in the day, with the king as sun and the queen as moon. Others think the king is Henry VIII, the queen Catherine, the maid Anne Boleyn. Still others believe it is about the first English Bible, with the blackbirds being the letters of the alphabet. Of course there are 26 letters—and 24 blackbirds. A recipe, published in 1598, describes a pie made "that the Birds be alive in them and flie out when it is cut up."

With zest

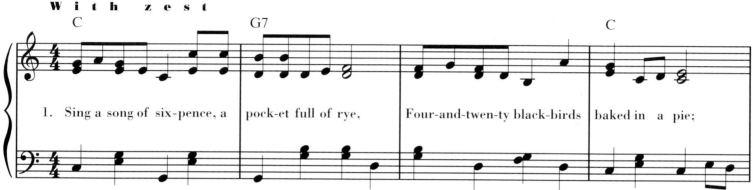

1. Sing a song of six-pence, a pock-et full of rye, Four-and-twen-ty black-birds baked in a pie;

When the pie was o-pened, the birds be-gan to sing, Was-n't that a dain-ty dish to set be-fore the King?

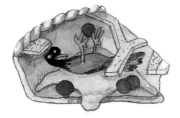

2. The King was in his counting house, counting out his money,

The Queen was in the parlor, eating bread and honey,

The maid was in the garden hanging out the clothes.

Along came a blackbird and nipped off her nose!

55

There Was a Crooked Man

There is some belief that this silly song refers to General Sir Alexander Leslie of Scotland, who worked out an agreement with King Charles I of England over the Scottish border—"the crooked stile."

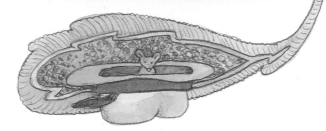

Happily

There was a crook-ed man and he walked a crook-ed mile, He

found a crook-ed six - pence up - on a crook-ed stile, He bought a crook-ed cat which

caught a crook-ed mouse, And they all lived to-geth-er in a lit - tle crook-ed house.

57

London Bridge

The game played with this little song, as well as the song itself, is both ancient and widespread. In Germany, the bridge is Magdeburg Bridge. In France and in Ireland versions of the song and the game even refer to the Devil. Scholars think the rhyme celebrates ancient rituals of sacrifice at the building of a bridge.

1. Lon - don Bridge is fall - ing down, fall - ing down, fall - ing down,

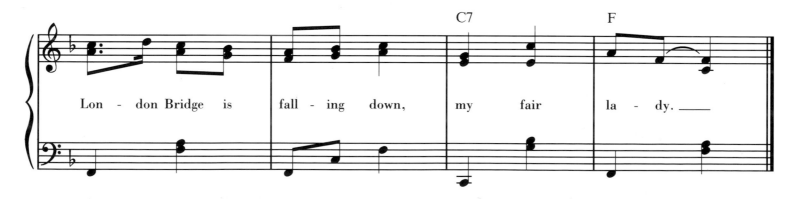

Lon - don Bridge is fall - ing down, my fair la - dy. _____

2. Build it up with iron bars, etc.

3. Iron bars will break and bend, etc.

4. Build it up with needles and pins, etc.

5. Pins and needles rust and bend, etc.

6. Build it up with gravel and stone, etc.

7. Gravel and stone will wash away, etc.

8. Build it up with silver and gold, etc.

9. Gold and silver will be stolen away, etc.

10. Then we'll set a man to watch, etc.

59

Mary Had a Little Lamb

Written in 1830 by Mrs. Sarah Josepha Hale of Boston, this nursery song was first published in a magazine called *Juvenile Miscellany*, which she edited.

Gaily

1. Mar - y had a lit - tle lamb, lit - tle lamb, lit - tle lamb,

Mar - y had a lit - tle lamb, Its fleece was white as snow.

2. And ev'rywhere that Mary went,
   Mary went, Mary went,
   Ev'rywhere that Mary went
   The lamb was sure to go.

3. It followed her to school one day,
   School one day, school one day,
   It followed her to school one day
   Which was against the rule.

4. It made the children laugh and play,
   Laugh and play, laugh and play,
   It made the children laugh and play
   To see a lamb at school.

5. And so the teacher turned it out,
   Turned it out, turned it out,
   And so the teacher turned it out
   But still it lingered near.

6. And waited patiently about,
   'Ly about, 'ly about,
   Waited patiently about,
   For Mary to appear.

7. "Why does the lamb love Mary so,
   Mary so, Mary so?
   Why does the lamb love Mary so?"
   The eager children cry.

8. "Why, Mary loves the lamb, you know,
   Lamb, you know, lamb, you know.
   Why, Mary loves the lamb, you know,"
   The teacher did reply.

61

Michael Finnigin

This popular Anglo-American game song just aches for new verses to be made up on the spot.

Brightly

1. There once was a man named Mi-chael Fin-ni-gin, He grew whis-kers on his chin-ni-gan, The

wind came out and blew them in a-gain, Poor old Mi-chael Fin-ni-gin. (Be-gin-ni-gin.)

2. There once was a man named Michael Finnigin,

   He kicked up an awful dinigin,

   Because they said he must not sinigin,

   Poor old Michael Finnigin. (Beginnigin.)

3. There was a man named Michael Finnigin,

   Climbed a tree and barked his shinigin,

   Took off several yards of skinigin,

   Poor old Michael Finnigin. (Beginnigin.)

The Little Nut Tree

A British political verse, this little rhyme may be about mad Juana, daughter of the king of Spain, who visited the court of Henry VII in 1506. Or it may be about Charles I of England, who had the gold and silver of England and was therefore considered by the Spanish king a great marriage catch for his young daughter. No one knows for sure.

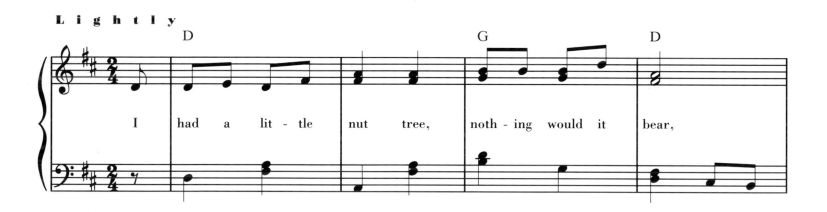

I had a lit - tle nut tree, noth - ing would it bear,

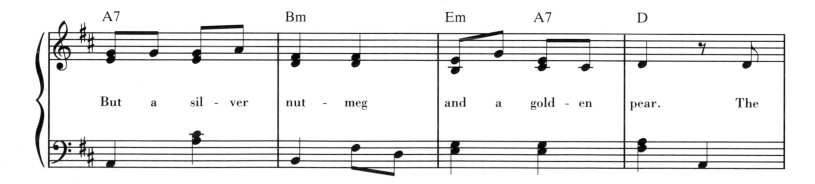

But a sil - ver nut - meg and a gold - en pear. The

64

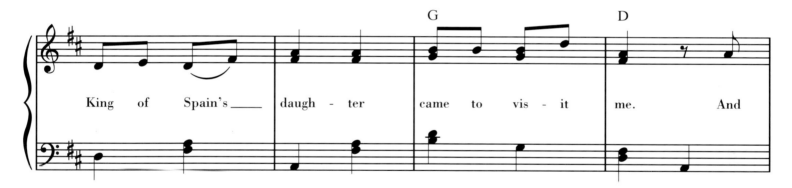

King of Spain's ___ daugh - ter came to vis - it me. And

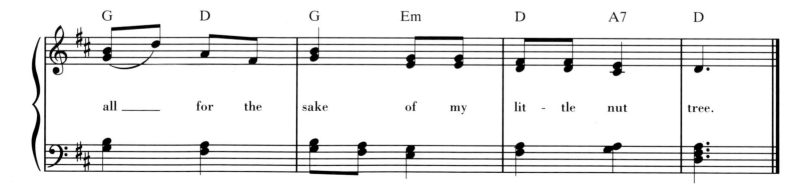

all ___ for the sake of my lit - tle nut tree.

The North Wind Doth Blow

This verse was originally an English weather rhyme. The robin referred to is not the American robin redbreast, but a British variety that stays around all winter long.

Gently

The North wind doth blow, And we shall have snow, And __ what will poor ro - bin do then, poor thing, poor thing?

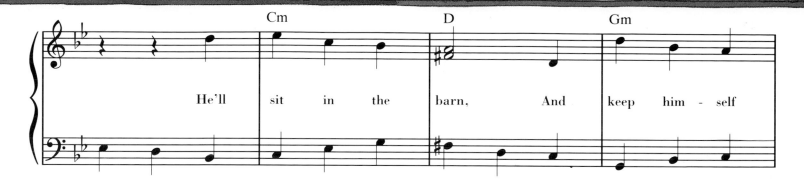

He'll sit in the barn, And keep him-self

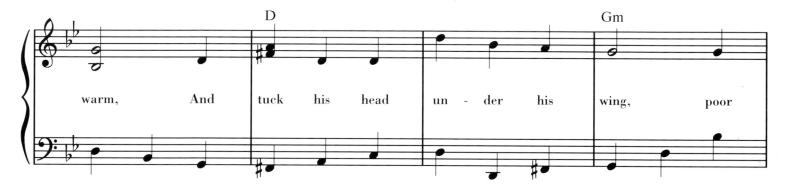

warm, And tuck his head un - der his wing, poor

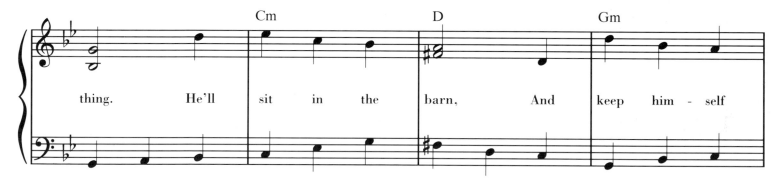

thing. He'll sit in the barn, And keep him-self

warm, And tuck his head un - der his wing. _____

Oats, Peas, Beans

A traditional British singing circle game, this nursery rhyme is a favorite in preschools. It changed into a counting-out rhyme in America's Midwest: "Oats, peas, beans, and barley corn, 'Tis you that's it on this fair morn."

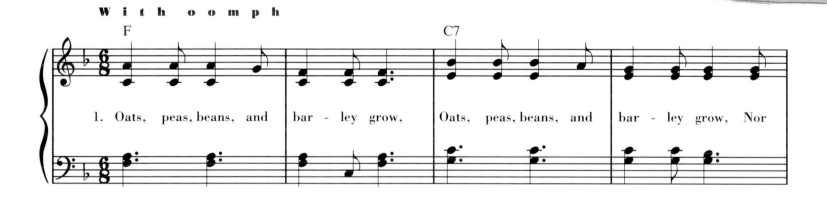

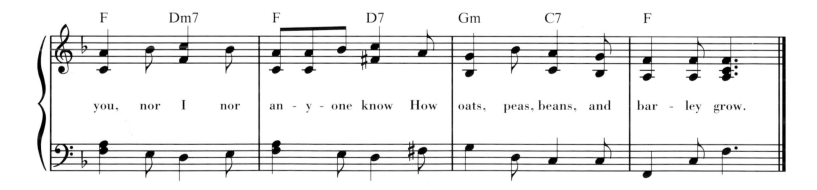

2. First the farmer sows his seeds,

    Then he stands and takes his ease,

    Stamps his feet, and claps his hands,

    And turns around to view the land.

3. Next the farmer waters the seeds,

    Stands erect. . . . . etc.

4. Next the farmer hoes the weeds,

    Stands erect. . . . etc.

5. Last the farmer harvests his seeds,

    Stands erect. . . . . . etc.

Old King Cole

The first time this song saw print was in 1708 in a philosophical treatise. The king referred to is the Cole who ruled Britain in the third century. He was reputedly a brave and popular man.

With zest

Old King Cole was a mer-ry old soul, And a mer-ry old soul was he. He

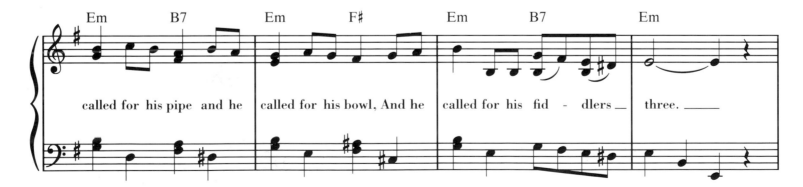

called for his pipe and he called for his bowl, And he called for his fid - dlers three.

Ev - 'ry _ fid - dler _ had . a _ fid-dle, and a ver - y fine _ fid-dle had _ he; _____ Twee-dle

dee, twee-dle dee, went the fid - dlers _ three, And _ mer - ry we _ will _ be. _____

Seesaw, Marjorie Daw

A song sung by children playing on a seesaw or teeter-totter, this song originally may have been sung by sawyers to help them keep up a proper rhythm on a two-handle saw.

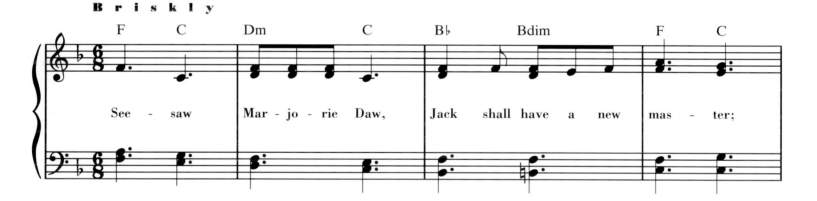

See - saw Mar - jo - rie Daw, Jack shall have a new mas - ter;

He shall have but a pen - ny a day, Be - cause he can't work an - y fast - er.

My Dame Hath a Lame, Tame Crane

An English round, this tongue twister is one of many used 100 years ago to help teach schoolchildren to pronounce words properly. This particular tongue tangler was written by Matthew White in 1630.

With a lilt

My | Dame hath a lame, tame crane. | My | Dame hath a crane that is lame. | Pray,

gen - tle Jane, take my crane that is lame, | And go home a - gain.

73

Oranges and Lemons

There are many versions of this famous song, though the earliest printing of it occurred in 1788. The bells referred to are all church bells in London or surrounding towns. The song is part of a children's game that ends with a tug-of-war to see whether the *oranges* or the *lemons* will win.

Smoothly

Or - an - ges and lem - ons, Say the bells of St. Clem - ents; You

owe me five far - things, Say the bells of St. Mar - tins; ____

74

When will you pay me? Say the bells of Old Bai - ley; ____

When I grow rich, Say the bells of Shore - ditch;

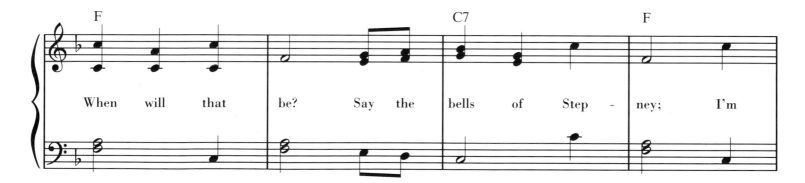

When will that be? Say the bells of Step - ney; I'm

sure   I   don't   know,   Says the   Great   Bell   of   Bow.

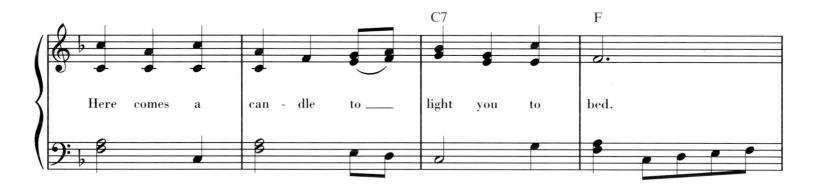

Here   comes   a   can - dle   to ____ light   you   to   bed.

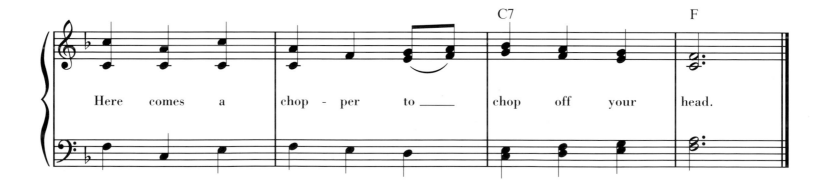

Here   comes   a   chop - per   to ____ chop   off   your   head.

Pease Porridge Hot

Pease porridge is a thin pudding made out of pease meal. Parts of this little rhyme were first published in the 1760s in Newbery's *Mother Goose's Melody*. Today, as in days past, the song accompanies a clapping game.

Gaily

1. Pease por-ridge hot,
   Pease por-ridge cold,
   Pease por-ridge in the pot,
   Nine days old.

2. Some like it hot,
   Some like it cold,
   Some like it in the pot,
   Nine days old.

Three Blind Mice

his traditional British round has been called "the best-known round in the world." A version was printed in 1609 by Thomas Ravenscroft.

With a bounce

Three blind mice, _____ three blind mice, _____

See how they run, _____ See how they run! _____ They

all ran af-ter the farm-er's wife, She cut off their tails with a carv - ing knife, Did you

ev - er see such a sight in your life as three blind mice?

There Was a Man and He Was Mad

There are both British and American versions of this song. This version is from Ohio. The first printings of any of the versions are from the 19th century.

With gathering force

1. There was a man and he was mad, And he jumped in-to the pud-ding bag.

2. The pudding bag it was so fine,
   That he jumped into a bottle of wine.

3. The bottle of wine it was so clear,
   He jumped into a bottle of beer.

4. The bottle of beer it was so thick,
   He jumped into a walking stick.

5. The walking stick it was so narrow,
   He jumped into a wheelbarrow.

6. The wheelbarrow it did so crack,
   He jumped onto a horse's back.

7. The horse's back it was so rotten
   He jumped into a bag of cotton.

8. The bag of cotton it set on fire
   And blew him up to Jeremiah.

(*spoken*)

Pouf! Pouf! Pouf!

81

There Was an Old Woman

The words of this song come from a sassy political song meant to ridicule King Henry V, who was leading his troops into battle against the French, what some saw as an impossible task. In fact, he won decisively, and the rhyme migrated into the nursery as a nonsense poem. The tune is the historical Irish song "Lilliburlero," which was sung in the 17th century with very angry political words.

With a bounce

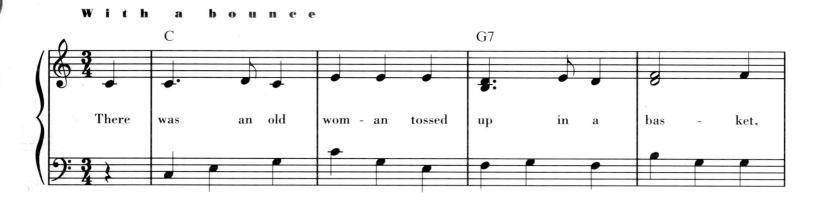

There was an old wom - an tossed up in a bas - ket,

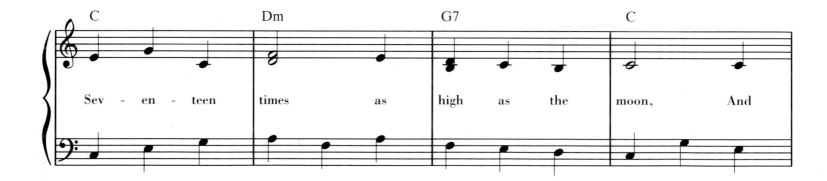

Sev - en - teen times as high as the moon, And

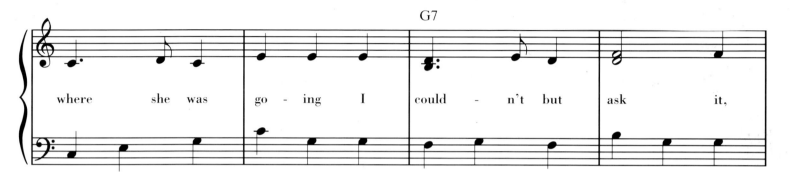

where she was go - ing I could - n't but ask it,

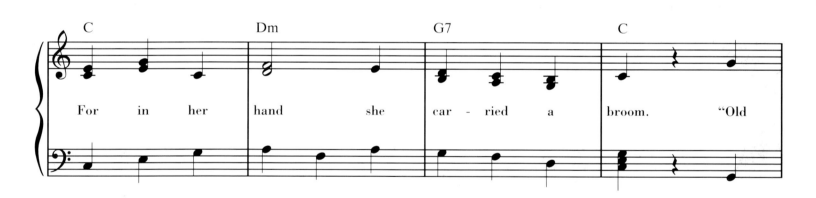

For in her hand she car - ried a broom. "Old

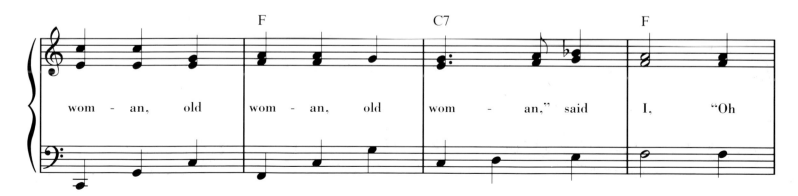

wom - an, old wom - an, old wom - an," said I, "Oh

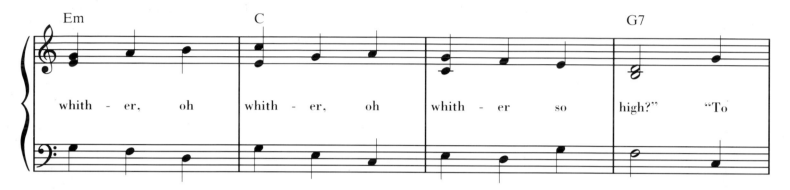

whith - er, oh whith - er, oh whith - er so high?" "To

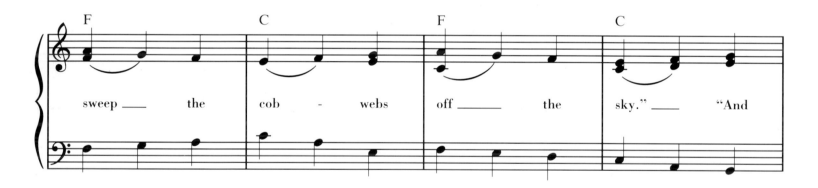

sweep ___ the cob - webs off ___ the sky." ___ "And

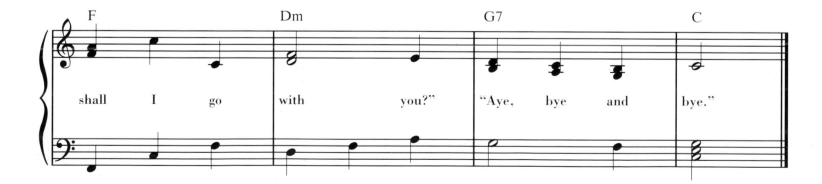

shall I go with you?" "Aye, bye and bye."

Tom, Tom, the Piper's Son

First appearing in a chap-book published in the 18th century, this rhyme is not about a real pig, but a pastry pig hawked by the "pig pye man" on the streets of English cities. Made of dough, with currants for eyes, these pigs had bellies filled with currants.

Quickly

G — Tom, Tom, the Pi-per's son,

C — Am — D — Stole a pig and a-way he run. The

G — G7 — pig got eat, and

C — Cm — Tom got beat, and

D7 — he went cry-ing

G — D — G — down the street.

This Old Man

game song from the North Country of England that goes back to the 18th century, this rollicking song took on a new popularity in the 1950s when it was sung in the movie *The Inn of the Sixth Happiness*.

Briskly

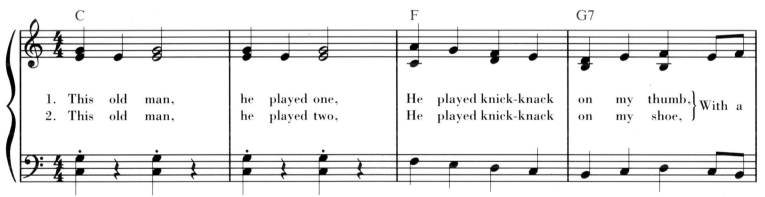

1. This old man, he played one, He played knick-knack on my thumb, With a
2. This old man, he played two, He played knick-knack on my shoe,

knick-knack, pad-dy wack, give the dog a bone, This old man came roll-ing home.

3. This old man, he played three,

   He played knick-knack on my knee,

   With a knick-knack, . . .etc.

4. This old man, he played four,

   He played knick-knack on my door,

   With a knick-knack, . . .etc.

5. This old man, he played five,

   He played knick-knack on my hive,

   With a knick-knack, . . .etc.

6. This old man, he played six,

   He played knick-knack on my sticks,

   With a knick-knack, . . .etc.

7. This old man, he played seven,

   He played knick-knack up to Heaven,

   With a knick-knack, . . .etc.

8. This old man, he played eight,

   He played knick-knack on my gate,

   With a knick-knack, . . .etc.

9. This old man, he played nine,

   He played knick-knack on my vine,

   With a knick-knack, . . .etc.

10. This old man, he played ten,

    He played knick-knack over again,

    With a knick-knack, . . .etc.

87

Who Killed Cock Robin?

The earliest mention of this dramatic nursery song is in *Tommy Thumb's Pretty Song Book*, published in London in 1744. There is, however, a stained-glass window dating from the 15th century at Buckland Rectory that depicts the same rhyme. The "bull" is also a bird—the bullfinch.

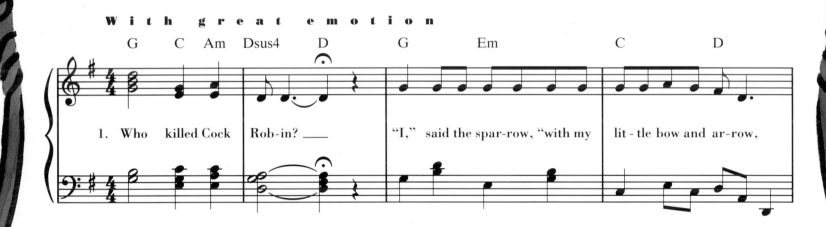

With great emotion

1. Who killed Cock Rob-in? ___ "I," said the spar-row, "with my lit-tle bow and ar-row,

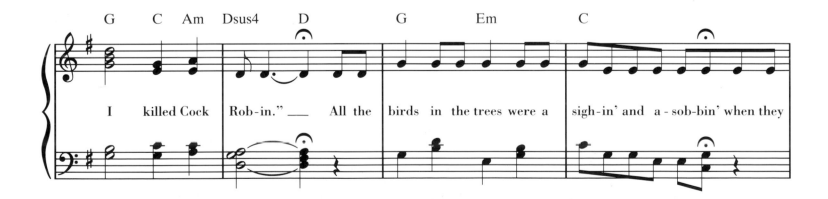

I killed Cock Rob-in." ___ All the birds in the trees were a sigh-in' and a-sob-bin' when they

heard of the death of | poor Cock Rob-in, When they | heard of the death of __ | poor Cock | Rob-in. __

2. Who saw him die?

"I," said the fly,

"With my teensy, weensy eye,

I saw him die." (Chorus)

3. Who'll dig his grave?

"I," said the owl,

"With my shovel and my trowel,

I'll dig his grave." (Chorus)

4. Who'll be the parson?

"I," said the rook,

"With my little bell and book,

I'll be the parson." (Chorus)

5. Who'll toll the bell?

"I," said the bull,

"Because I can pull,

I'll toll the bell." (Chorus)

Three Little Kittens

This nursery song was first published in 1843 by Eliza Follen in her book *New Nursery Songs for All Good Children.*

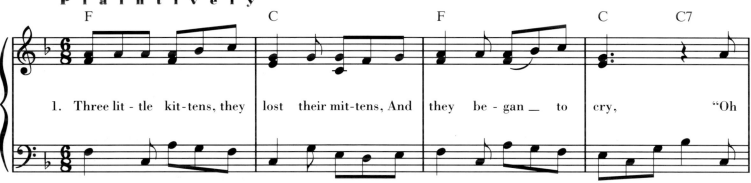

Plaintively

F   C   F   C   C7

1. Three lit - tle kit-tens, they lost their mit-tens, And they be - gan — to cry, "Oh

B♭   C7   Am   Dm   C7   F

Moth - er, dear, — we sad - ly fear, — Our mit - tens we — have lost." (Spoken) "What?

Lost your mit-tens? You naugh - ty kit-tens, Then you shall have no pie. Me-

ow, _____ Me - ow, _____ Then you shall have _ no pie."

2. Three little kittens, they found their mittens,

And they began to cry,

"Oh, Mother, dear, see here, see here,

Our mittens we have found."

"What? Found your mittens?

You lovely kittens,

Then you shall have some pie."

"Me-ow, Me-ow, then we shall have some pie!"

Twinkle, Twinkle, Little Star

An old and popular nursery rhyme by Jane Taylor, this was set to music many times, but the melody with the greatest staying power was originally written by Mozart in 1778.

Gently

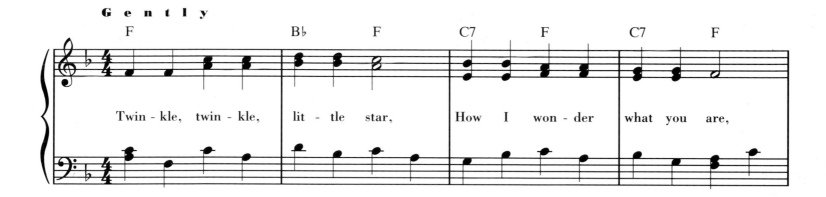

Twin - kle, twin - kle, lit - tle star, How I won - der what you are,

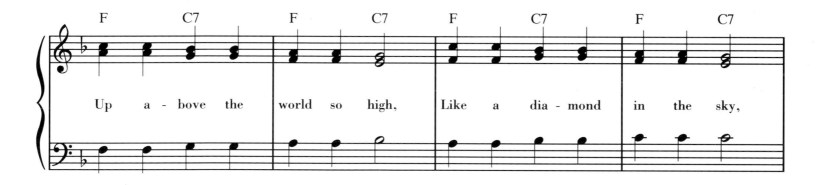

Up a - bove the world so high, Like a dia - mond in the sky,

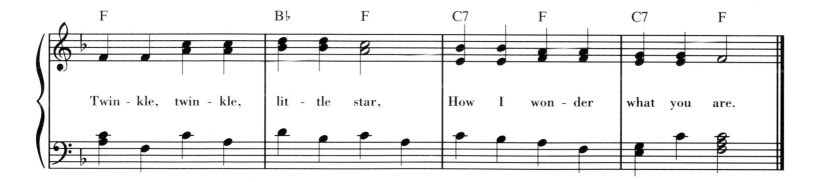

Twin - kle, twin - kle, lit - tle star, How I won - der what you are.

Index

Jane Yolen is the author of more than one hundred books, including the Caldecott Medal winner *Owl Moon*, illustrated by John Schoenherr. She has been the recipient of the Kerlan Award for her body of work as well as the 1992 Regina Medal from the Catholic Library Association. Her other music books include *Rounds About Rounds* and *The Fireside Song Book of Birds and Beasts* with Barbara Green and three books with Adam Stemple. She has been on the board of directors of the Society of Children's Book Writers since its inception. Her books for Boyds Mills Press include *Street Rhymes Around the World*, *An Invitation to the Butterfly Ball*, and *All in the Woodland Early*. She lives in Hatfield, Massachusetts.

Adam Stemple is a member of a Minneapolis-based band, POETIC JUSTICE, and is a composer as well as a guitarist and keyboard player. His previous books with his mother, Jane Yolen, are *The Lullaby Songbook*, *Hark! A Christmas Sampler*, and *The Lap-Time Song & Play Book*. He also collaborated with Naomi Kojima on a book published in Japan. He lives in Minneapolis, Minnesota.

Rosekrans Hoffman is a painter turned illustrator whose works have been exhibited in several museums, including the Whitney Museum and the Brooklyn Museum. She has written two children's books and illustrated more than twenty. She recently returned to Nebraska, her home state, with her husband and black cat.